Diary of an Unbroken Heart

Simple Keys for Making Complex Changes

Diary of an Unbroken Heart

Simple Keys for Making Complex Changes

By Janeé Hill

ISBN - 978-0692838655

Book design and layout: Russell Lake, SeedStudios.com

DISCLAIMER: The names, dates, and occurrences have been modified to protect the individuals involved.

Dedication

Diary of an Unbroken Heart is dedicated to my incredible family, who truly loves me like Jesus with skin on. I am so grateful for each of you and your ongoing love and support. Thank you for believing in me when there wasn't much to believe in.

To Ed and Valerie Riefenstahl and Debbie Rasa, thank you for walking me through some really dark, difficult times and for helping me see the beautiful rainbow at the end.

To my spunky friend Katy Slayton, who inspired me to finish this book, may your legacy of love, service and leadership live on.

To my Savior and Lord, Jesus Christ, thank you for *all* you have brought me through and for creating me for "such a time as this."

Contents

Introduction

Are you ready to experience life to the fullest? Is pain from your past impacting your joy in the present? Have you given up on some of your dreams, not wanting to be disappointed with another failed attempt? Are you firing on all cylinders yet still feel like there must be more to life?

If you answered "Yes" to any (or all) of the above, this book is for you! *Diary of an Unbroken Heart* walks you through 13 simple strategies for making complex changes in your life. This book isn't based on studies, science or clinical psychiatry. While all of those areas are important, and sometimes necessary, my book is about experience. It offers practical and proven (by me!) steps I've taken to turn my life around.

WHAT? You turned your life around? You mean you haven't always been a happy, purpose-filled woman of God who thrives on helping others and being a positive role model? you may wonder. Nope. I have not. In fact, I was just the opposite.

I was a self-serving, manipulative, broken woman struggling to find her way. From the outside, people may have thought I had it altogether. I had a great job, ran in the right circles, wore the most fabulous clothes. But on the inside, I was fighting serious insecurities, depression, addiction, etc. I had been through a lot in my life—childhood sexual abuse, domestic violence, multiple heartbreaks—

the list goes on and on. My life felt like one issue after another, and I *never* thought I would break free of these cycles.

Now, by the grace of God (and through a lot of hard work), I am living a life full of freedom, passion, purpose and true happiness. And you can too! Fair warning here: this journey isn't for the faint of heart. I transparently bare some of my deepest hurts and feelings through some of the diary entries shared in this book (note: the names and actual dates have been changed to protect anonymity). My hope and prayer is that my authenticity will inspire you to let down the walls and really deal with some things once and for all. Picking up any broken pieces in our lives and crafting them into a beautiful mosaic of bygones takes rigorous honesty, commitment and the desire to change. Embrace the process.

My suggestion for working through *Diary of an Unbroken Heart* is to complete one 'Key' a week. You might have noticed I said you'll be "**working** through this book." That's correct! This book is an easy read, but it won't be an easy process. And it shouldn't be. Don't speed-read the text or blow through the assignments. You've spent decades becoming who you are today. There's no overnight fix to becoming the person you deserve to be and can be. Making lasting changes is hard, but I'll say it again. You can do it!

My hope is that together, you and I will laugh, cry, grow and throw the door wide open to all the great things God has in store for us.

Anything is possible if you believe.

Let your journey begin!

Janeé

The Power of Choice

Dear Diary,   *January 16, 2006*

I'm so confused. Why, why, why do I keep doing this? It's always something. What's wrong with me? I promised myself that I would not have more than one glass of wine. Next thing I knew, I was three sheets to the wind and saying all kinds of things to be the life of the party.

It's a sign of a bigger problem, I know. I'm just not happy. I'm making bad decisions trying to make myself happier. But I should be happy! I have a good job, great boyfriend, and a closet full of rockin' Jimmy Choos. I live in the best neighborhood in town and travel the world on a whim with a girl squad Taylor Swift would kill for. I have great parents who believe in me, even though I am far from the girl they believe me to be. And I have my whole life ahead of me and a world of possibilities. Why do I continue to self-sabotage?

*I can't shake my insecurities, my rocky past,
my bad moves, on and on. Will anything ever make
me happy? The yoga, meditation, therapy and
prescription meds aren't working. Maybe I should
downward dog my way to a higher dose. Move?
Switch jobs? Find a new guy? How am I ever going to
be happy?*

*I swear, I'm so over this feeling. I want out of
this rut. No, I really want out of this life.*

Dictionary.com defines the word choice as: "the right, power, or opportunity to choose."

YOU have the *right,* the *power* and the *opportunity* to choose to change. Read that again, this time with meaning! It's a powerful statement. It's also completely underutilized.

Let's assume you're of sound mind, even though you might not feel like it right now. YOU can choose to change whatever it is you don't like about yourself or your life. YOU can change what isn't working.

I can hear you already: "Janeé, you don't understand how long I have been struggling with *this.*" or "Janeé, you have no idea how much I've been through and how hurt I am." My favorite is "Janeé, this will never change." Uh, uh, sister. No excuses. Remember: YOU have the *right,* the *power* and the *opportunity* to choose to change.

And I understand. I've been there. A neighbor sexually abused me at a very young age. Shortly after that, I developed petit mal seizures and was put on a high-powered medication, which caused me to gain weight. Embarrassed of what I had been through and what I looked like, I began making up stories about myself to try to get people to like me. This pattern continued for many, many years and led me to feel even worse about myself. To counteract how I was feeling, I developed some pretty bad vices (e.g., an eating disorder, abusing prescription medications, and trying to drink myself to death). Later in life, I got a handle on the vices and the lying, but my reality did not improve. I married a "pastor," got pregnant on our honeymoon, and shortly after, became a victim of domestic violence. When he was arrested for assault with bodily injury (I was the one assaulted), I discovered he had a prior criminal record and had served years in jail for charges related to both theft and fraud. My life went from bad to worse to absolute hell. I delivered my son stillborn, and the marriage was annulled four days later on the basis of fraud. I spent the next few years alone trying to deal (and heal) from what seemed like a life-long heartache.

Fast forward through years of hard work, and we arrive at today. By the grace of God I have a life I never thought possible; my past no longer haunts me. I walk in freedom from bad choices (most of the time), as well as addictive behaviors and patterns. I have peace where I used to have panic. I have self-love and laughter where I used to have self-loathing and loneliness. You deserve that too.

So how do we do it? Remember our little friend "choice?" For me, it started with two choices I made in 2007.

The first choice I made was to change how I lived. Before 2007, I was a fake, and a good one. On the outside, I looked successful. I had a growing career and an expensive car. I carried a megawatt smile and a gorgeous Prada handbag. But on the inside, I was a certified hot mess, with the emphasis on "mess." I pretended to be someone I wasn't. I struggled to pay bills and have meaningful relationships. I also tried to end my life.

But I did have a career as a motivational speaker, and in 2007, I was asked to speak to some high school girls about professional etiquette. Instead of etiquette, the conversation "mysteriously" took a very different turn. For the first time in public, I spoke about being sexually abused as a child. I was shaking after my speech, wondering if I'd gone too far and shared too much. But something unexpected happened. Two teenage girls told me that they, too, had been sexually abused. Then and there, I realized that sharing my hurt, in an honest and real way, could help other people.

For the first time in my life, I made the choice to change, truly change. 'Truly' was the key; to me it meant once and for all. I wanted to live an honest, authentic life that helped others. But how? Was it too little too late, after all I had been through and all of the mistakes I had made?

It is *never* too late to be the person you were destined to be. How do you do that? The answer lies in the second choice I made that day, which I will discuss in the next chapter.

Enough about me. Are you ready to *choose* to make changes in your life? I realize the changes I wanted (and needed) to make were sizable. Maybe you don't see yours as quite that big, but they *are* changes you know you want to make. Are you ready? Are you willing to let go of your past and allow yourself to experience joy, both now and in the future? If so, congratulations! Your first exercise is below.

If you feel you aren't ready right now to choose, that's okay. Tuck this book away until you are, or give it to someone else who is ready. It has been my experience that self-help books do very little to move us forward until we are ready to help ourselves.

Courage to Change - Exercise One

1. Write down the changes in your life you'd like to make and why. List every one you can think of. Try to do this quickly, so your pen or pencil never stops moving. Leave space at the end of every listed change. You might want to add to your thoughts later.

_____

_____

_____

_____

_____

_____

_____

2. How are each of the changes you listed above negatively affecting you? Rank them in order below, from worst offender to least offender. Feel free to add additional changes as they come to mind.

3. Why is it important for you to make the changes listed above?
    Don't speed through this question. Think it through, taking time
    to be honest with yourself. _____

    _____

    _____

    _____

    _____

    _____

    _____

    _____

    _____

    _____

    _____

    _____

    _____

    _____

    _____

    _____

    _____

    _____

    _____

    _____

    _____

    _____

    _____

    _____

4. How do you imagine your life will improve after making these changes? _____

_____

_____

_____

_____

_____

_____

_____

_____

_____

_____

_____

_____

_____

_____

_____

_____

_____

_____

_____

_____

_____

_____

_____

_____

_____

_____

_____

5. If you choose to make the above changes in your life, write yourself a letter of commitment. It's for your eyes only, and there is no preferred format. State the changes you'll make and why you'll make them, as well as the expected improvements to your life. (Yes, I know you just did this, but accountability calls! You'll take this commitment more seriously if you've promised yourself to do it.)

_____

_____

_____

_____

_____

_____

_____

_____

_____

_____

_____

_____

_____

_____

_____

_____

_____

_____

_____

_____

_____

_____

"I cannot change my past, but I can choose to change my future." – Janeé Hill

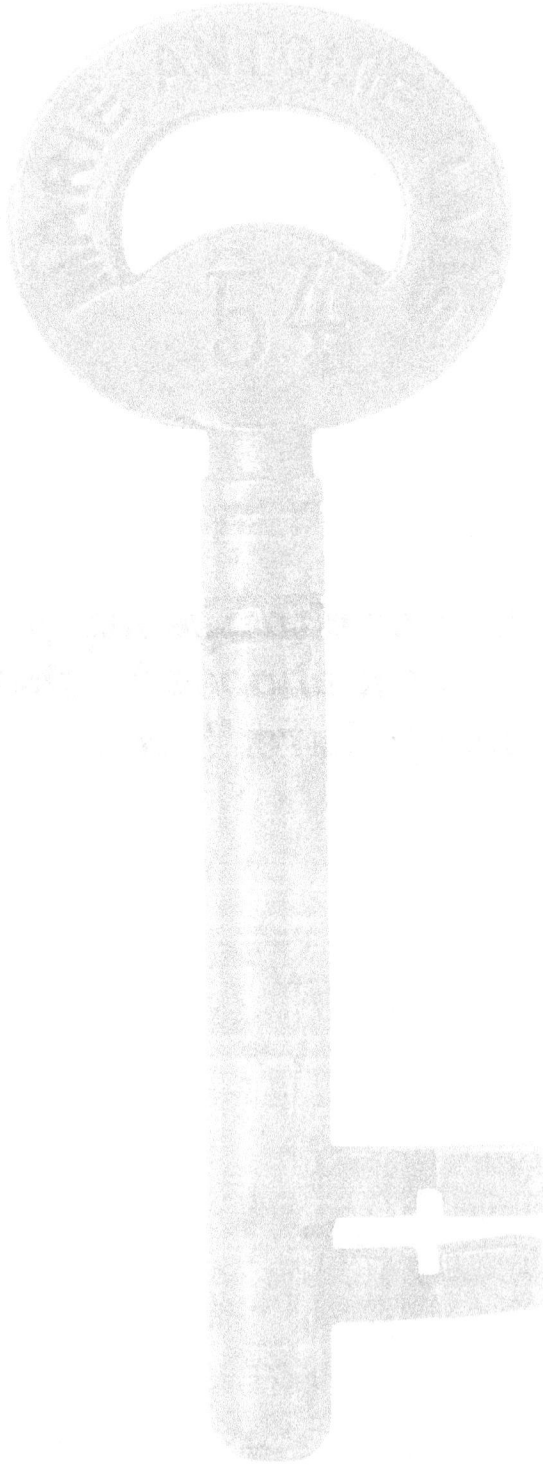

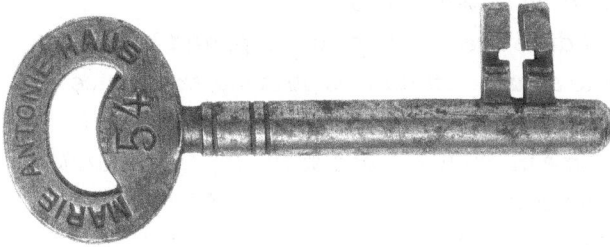

Key Two

Believe!

Dear Diary,   June 9, 2007

    Earlier today, I spoke to a group of teenage "debutantes." I use quotation marks because while that was the audience I was told to expect, that wasn't the audience I got. I went in prepared, with a speech polished to perfection. I'd been a debutante growing up, so I knew these girls: wealthy, well-poised, educated and articulate.

    Um, yeah, no. The girls in front of me were the opposite of what I expected. They were underprivileged, rough around the edges, street-taught young ladies that a pastor's wife deemed "debutantes" in an effort to give them a privileged identity in their new relationship with Jesus Christ. I was supposed to speak to these girls on dining etiquette, but the conversation took a very different turn.

    At the end of my talk, I asked the girls what questions they had, and one asked, "If a guy asks *you out, who pays?" I said, "He does, but that doesn't mean you owe him anything." Another girl then asked, "What if he doesn't take 'No' for an answer?"*

Wow! I didn't see that one coming, and before I knew it, I was sharing with these girls my experience of being sexually assaulted when I was a child. And for the first time in my life, I was speaking openly and honestly about this. FOR THE FIRST TIME IN MY LIFE. I told them the abuse led me to make decisions against myself throughout most of my life. As a result of my transparency, several of the girls started sharing—many for the first time—about sexual abuse they had experienced and how they wanted to stop the cycle of allowing men to take advantage of them.

I left that speaking engagement with a totally different perspective on my life. It's hard to believe, but it's true. What if God actually allowed these things to happen to me so that one day I could share with others? What if my voice could keep others from being victims? What if I could turn my life around and deal with the pain of my past once and for all? Is that even possible???

Before this entry in my diary, I thought my life was a mistake. Even as an adult, I didn't quite fit in, and I certainly wasn't comfortable in my own skin. I had successfully dazzled the outside world with my great job, embarrassing wealth of material items, community groups joined and fancy events attended. BUT, on the inside, I was desolate. I tried multiple times to kill myself, battled bouts of addiction, entered into toxic relationships, and a laundry list of other bad moves on my part.

Though I tried, nothing could fill the void in me, and nothing would stop the unending pain. Nothing, that is, except the unending love of Jesus Christ.

Over time I came to realize the only thing that could, and did, fill my void in my heart and life was a relationship with Jesus Christ. Only He can turn our pain into purpose, our mess into a masterpiece, our loss into a life worth living. I know this because of my life experiences. The Bible's promises are spot on.

I grew up in a conservative Christian home. My parents loved the Lord and took me to church whenever the doors were open (at least, that's what it felt like). I asked Jesus to become my Lord and Savior when I was 8 years old, and I knew He was in my heart from that point on. For many years, however, my faith was based on religious practices instead of a personal relationship. During that time, I thought if I made a mistake or sinned (as we Christians like to call it), God would be mad at me, and He would no longer be my friend.

That couldn't be further from the truth. The truth is that God loves us, and He sent His Only Son, Jesus, to die on the cross for us. Three days later, Jesus rose from the dead. Now, He lives with God in heaven. And if we have accepted Him, we have the Holy Spirit in our hearts to guide, direct and protect us. Once I understood the idea of a relationship with Jesus versus religion, my life changed completely.

I never thought I could have real relationships built on honesty and trust. Now, I can't have them any other way.

I never thought I could have freedom from addictive thoughts and behaviors. Today, I'm unchained from any former vices (except maybe a small, succulent sweet treat at bedtime).

I never thought I could have a purposeful life that benefits others. I have now started a nonprofit to share the hope, help and healing power of Christ with others.

I never thought I could trust men again. Yet, here I am, remarried and the doting mom (to the nth degree) of our toddler son. And just so you know, he's the happiest, cutest, most loving little dude on the planet. Not that I'm biased or anything.

I never thought I could experience a truly fulfilled life. AND I DO! This fulfillment does not come from "things." Rather, it comes from having THE "thing," which, for me, is a relationship with Jesus Christ.

You can have a fulfilled life too! It is not an easy road. But it is definitely a road worth taking.

For me, the true path to progress began when I asked Jesus to come into my life and be my Lord and Savior. As I mentioned, I had "accepted" Jesus when I was a child, but it was more of a religious decision more than a relational choice. In 2007, when I re-dedicated my life to Him, I knew I had begun living for the first time.

Maybe you are ready to start a relationship with Jesus, or perhaps you would like to renew or change your relationship with Him. If so, it's easy. All you have to do is ask Jesus into your heart, and to be your Lord and Savior. Below is a simple prayer that could change your life forever.

> *Dear God,*
>
> *I know that I have messed up. I have made mistakes. I ask that you forgive me.*
>
> *Lord, I believe you sent your Son Jesus, to die for my sins. After three days, He rose again. And Jesus is now with you in heaven. If I believe in you, you will fill me with the Holy Spirit.*
>
> *Lord, I want a relationship with you. I want you to come in and be the Lord of my life. Amen.*

That's it. That's all you have to do. Don't worry about getting the words just right; simply talk to Him. He's ready to meet you wherever you are. And if you already have a relationship with Jesus Christ, but maybe haven't really communicated with Him in a while, that's okay. He's there for you too.

I want to make it clear that I'm not a Bible scholar. I don't even play one on TV. I'm simply a girl who loves Jesus and has felt His healing power firsthand. Despite my hurts and heartaches, I finally have, now and forever, an unbroken heart.

Courage to Change – Exercise Two

1. How do you view God? _____

    _____

    _____

    _____

    _____

    _____

    _____

    _____

    _____

    _____

    _____

    _____

    _____

    _____

    _____

    _____

    _____

    _____

2. What do you think and hope God wants for you and your life?

    _____

    _____

    _____

    _____

    _____

    _____

_____

_____

_____

_____

_____

_____

_____

_____

_____

_____

_____

3. Do you think God loves you? Why or why not?

_____

_____

_____

_____

_____

_____

_____

_____

_____

_____

_____

_____

_____

_____

_____

_____

4. The Bible talks about God's love for us. Read Romans 5:8 and
    8:31-39. What do you think about these passages?

_____

_____

_____

_____

_____

_____

_____

_____

_____

_____

_____

_____

_____

_____

_____

_____

_____

_____

_____

_____

_____

_____

_____

_____

_____

_____

_____

"For you created my inmost being; you knit me together in my mother's womb. I praise you because I am fearfully and wonderfully made; your works are wonderful, I know that full well." - Psalm 139:13-14

(New International Version)

Key Three

The Right Crew for the Improved You

Dear Diary,   *June 10, 2008*

I had lunch with Susie today. After spending time with her, I found myself super negative. I was really critical of myself and anyone else I encountered or who came to mind. Susie's a good friend, so supportive of me, but her pessimism wipes me out.

Separately, two days ago, a colleague suggested I meet this Christian woman. She thought she would be a good person for me to know. "Boy, this should be fun," I thought...."I am sure she is going to judge me for everything I have ever done in my life!!!!" But she didn't!!! I told her a little bit of my story (poor choices in my past – the lying, eating disorder, prescription meds and alcohol abuse), and instead of judging me or questioning me, she encouraged me! Right off the bat! Before we left the café, she even prayed for me and told me that she knew God had a great plan

*for my life. She also said that she would be a "lifer,"
meaning a life-long friend who would be with me as I
learn to do this thing called, "life," in a healthy way.*

*Is this for real? I'm totally inspired by her and
excited about the possibility of having a friend who
likes me for me, versus the person I pretended to be.*
WOW!

How many of us want to go through this scary process of "change" alone? Hmmm ... I don't think anyone is raising his or her hand. Why? Because we were not created to go through life alone, especially tough times, which you will encounter if you choose to change.

There are three kinds of people in our lives: Uppers, Downers, and Neutralizers. Yes, it does sound like we're talking about drugs here. We're not, but close. The way people make us feel can be drug-like. People can bring us up or people can bring us down. People who play no significant role in our lives I call Neutralizers.

It's my experience that we must have Uppers in our lives. These people support us, cheer for us, and notice our improvements, even when they're small. They also point out our blind spots, meaning areas or behaviors we'd probably change if we were aware of them. Uppers are people we can be ourselves with, and at the same time, they encourage us to better versions of ourselves. We heart them!

With the right people, our potential is limitless. They are always looking for the good in us.

Now, with the wrong people, the Downers, we can do no right. They will always find fault with us. Downers are the opposite of Uppers.

Years ago, I fired a contract employee. Afterward, one of my office interns said, "I don't know what she did that was bad. I just know I never felt good about myself when she was here." This is exactly what Downers do. They often leave us feeling bad about ourselves. In addition, they may tempt us to make bad choices because they want to have "bad behavior buddies." For instance, you are working hard to lose some weight, and a "Downer" friend might say, "You don't need to lose weight. Why don't you skip the gym today and head to 'happy hour' with me."

What about the people who are not moving us either forward or backward in life? There are two ways to look at Neutralizers. First, maybe they're an acquaintance or a relationship that doesn't require much energy from you. Joe, is my dry cleaner. From our conversations, he seems like a great guy. He's professional, friendly and always delivers my clothes in perfect fashion and on time. He and I have a pleasant relationship, but the relationship doesn't play a significant role in my life. (No offense meant here! I think Joe would say the same thing about me.) It's a much needed respite relationship, a low maintenance relationship. On the other hand, Neutralizers could be taking away from time spent with our Upper girls and guys. Let's say you really need to meet with your mentor aka an Upper. However, you choose to hang out at the pool with a Neutralizer instead. How do you think this decision will help move you forward?

Only you can determine if you are with the right crew (the friends who are like family to you). If you desire to move forward, ask yourself this question: is your crew helping you become an improved you?

Courage to Change – Exercise Three

1. List the Uppers in your life. How does each one make you feel and why?

    _____

    _____

    _____

    _____

    _____

    _____

    _____

    _____

    _____

    _____

    _____

    _____

    _____

    _____

    _____

    _____

    _____

2. Have you told your Uppers lately how important they are to you and why? If not, do so. _____

    _____

    _____

    _____

    _____

    _____

    _____

    _____

    _____

    _____

    _____

    _____

    _____

3. List the Downers in your life? How does each one make you feel and why? _____

_____

_____

_____

_____

_____

_____

_____

_____

_____

_____

_____

_____

_____

4. Why are you maintaining the Downer relationships? What are you getting out of the relationship? List each Downer and why you maintain the relationship. _____

_____

_____

_____

_____

_____

_____

_____

_____

_____

_____

_____

_____

_____

_____

_____

5. What can you do to lessen the impact of the Downers in your life? How will you set healthy boundaries? _____

_____

_____

_____

_____

_____

_____

_____

_____

_____

_____

_____

_____

_____

_____

_____

_____

_____

6. Are you an Upper to everyone you should be an Upper to? List the people to whom you owe some time, energy and support. Make a commitment to contact each person, and reach out in a genuine way. Call or visit—no emails or texts; make it personal. Follow up that conversation by doing something meaningful to help each person. _____

_____

_____

_____

_____

_____

_____

_____

"Do not be misled: Bad company corrupts good character." 1 Corinthians 15:33

(New International Version)

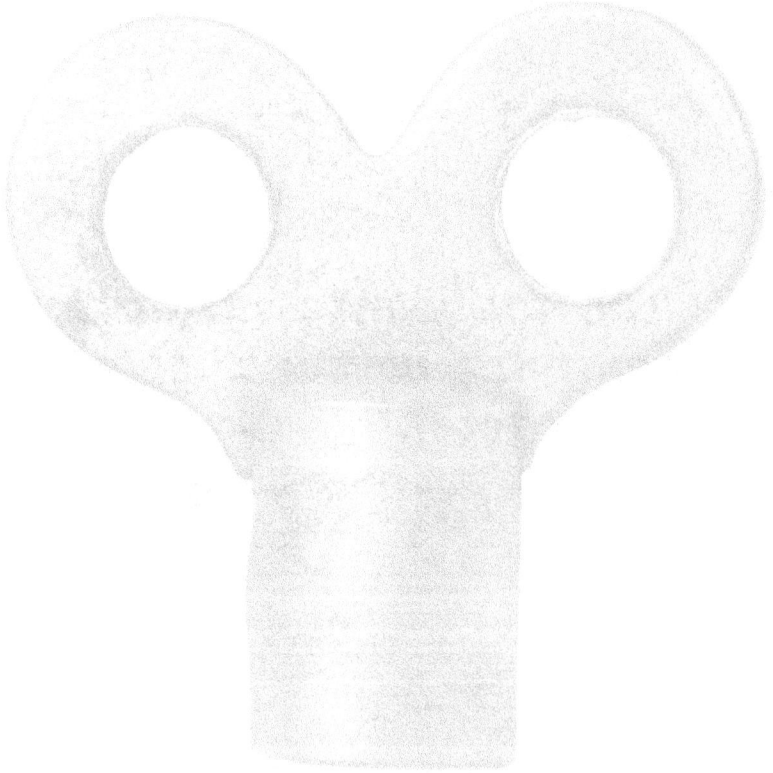

Key Four

Small Things = Big Changes

Dear Diary,   *March 20, 2009*

    I'm absolutely devastated. Can't stop crying and screaming. Bill committed suicide. He and I had been through the fire and back. We had similar struggles, similar personalities, and most importantly, we had both made similar, positive changes in our lives. Why would he do this?

    I called a mutual friend, hoping she could make me feel better; instead she made me feel worse. So much worse. It was like a slap in the face to hear her say I was no different than Bill. She told me my life was up and down, full of bad choices, and that I'll never really change. OUCH!

    Where was her venom coming from? And worse, was she right? Have I been kidding myself, again, to think I can actually put my past behind me for good?

*She is right! I have tried, in the past, to change. What
makes me think this time is any different???*
    But it IS different, I know that in my heart.
*While I cannot necessarily say why it is different,
or what is different, I truly know there are some big
changes going on inside of my life.*

Making big changes in our lives is daunting, especially if some of the people around us doubt our intentions or our chances of success.

Early on in my journey to change, I was making drastic and very public external changes, hoping other people would notice, and praise me. I gave away almost all of my designer clothes and accessories— yes, it was good to be my friend back then. I sold my solid (and so cute) luxury car and bought a broken-down 1993 Range Rover—one of the dumbest things ever. I chose YouTube as the place to announce to the world that I was changing. What was I thinking?!

What I learned from that external effort was that my internal wounds were still there. In some ways I felt worse because my once private struggles were now very public.

I also learned real change is a slow, often painful, process. Sorry to break it to you, folks. Change requires small, consistent steps in the right direction versus "one giant leap for mankind," as Neil Armstrong said about reaching the moon.

Think about it like this. A morbidly obese person undergoes gastric bypass—a major surgery that produces a major change. If he doesn't follow a healthy diet and exercise plan (small, consistent steps), he'll probably wind up back where he was.

On the other hand, if someone wants to lose weight and commits to consistently adding in a few fruits and vegetables daily, combined with exercise several times a week, she will be more likely to achieve the desired change, even though it will take longer. And chances are, she will keep the changes.

We live in an instant gratification society. However, it has been my experience that when I make small, consistent steps towards change, they always result in slow, but lasting, big changes. Change is a marathon, not a sprint.

Courage to Change – Exercise Four

1. What is a big change you want to make in life? This answer can be the same one you listed in Key One or it can be something different, if you've changed your mind.

_____

_____

_____

_____

_____

_____

_____

_____

_____

_____

_____

_____

_____

_____

_____

_____

_____

_____

_____

_____

_____

_____

2. What are some small, consistent steps you can take to accomplish the big change you want to make?

_____

_____

_____

_____

_____

_____

_____

_____

_____

_____

_____

_____

_____

_____

_____

_____

_____

_____

_____

_____

_____

_____

_____

_____

_____

_____

_____

_____

_____

_____

_____

_____

3. What potential obstacles or fears could get in the way of making these changes? How will you overcome them?

_____

_____

_____

_____

_____

_____

_____

_____

_____

_____

_____

_____

_____

_____

_____

_____

_____

4. Find a breakthrough buddy and talk to him (or her) about the changes you're making in your life. This will help hold you accountable to the changes you are seeking to make. A breakthrough buddy is a person you trust, who has your best interests in mind, and will support you through your commitment to change. A breakthrough buddy is one of your Uppers.

_____

_____

_____

_____

_____

_____

_____

_____

"Sometimes the smallest steps in the right direction end up being the biggest steps of your life. Tip toe if you must, but take the steps." – Author Unknown

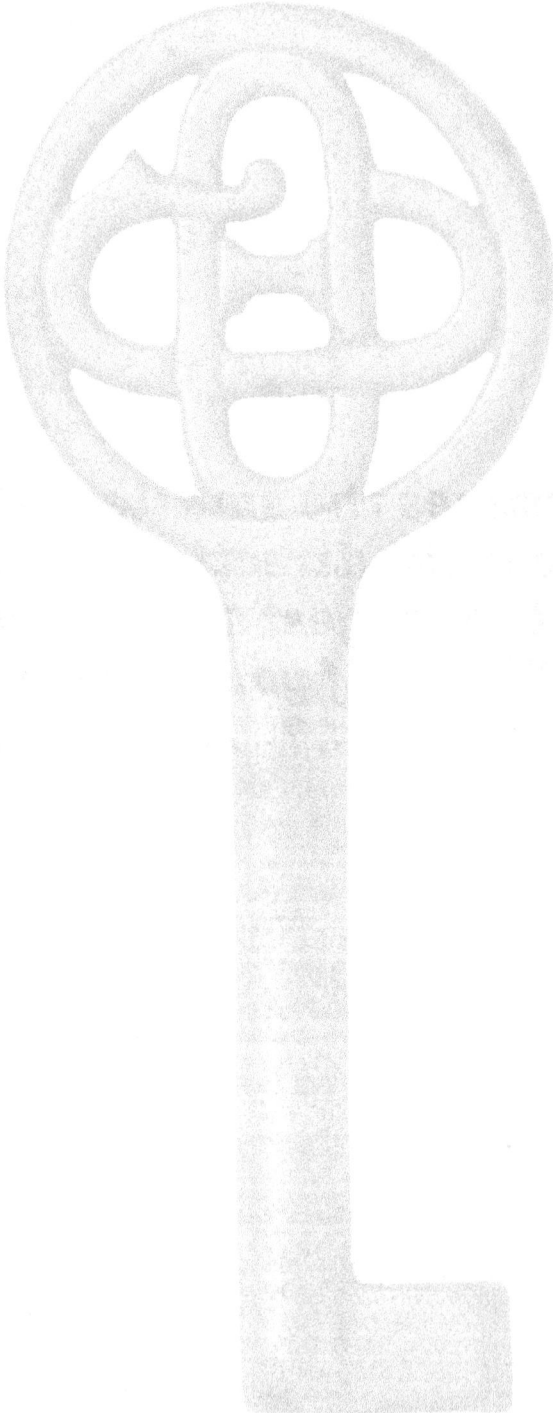

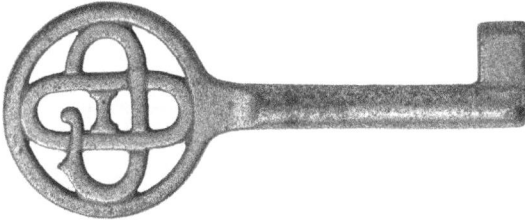

Comfortably Uncomfortable

Dear Diary, August 15, 2009

    Tonight's the night! My first attempt at stand-up comedy. My gig (I can use that word. I'm a professional now!) is at Addison Improv in Addison, Texas. It's open mic night and a bunch of friends are coming to laugh with me, or at me; I'm not sure! This seemed like a good idea at the time, but now ... eeek! Stand-up is something I've always wanted to try, but at this particular moment, I'm not sure why. It's quite a jump from motivational speaker to stand-up comedian.

    Speaking of jump, my TV producer-friend talked me into skydiving! I am terrified. I HATE heights! I am the girl who had to be pushed off of the bungee jump in South Padre because I stood on the platform for over an hour. How am I going to pull this one off? And

if I don't pull it off, the consequences are pretty scary
– DEATH!
But I love a challenge, and for me, these things
are super big challenges!!! So....let's do this!

If we want different results, we have to do different things. This means getting out of our comfort zones. It's a good thing that I'm settled by being "comfortably uncomfortable."

To me, stand-up comedy seemed like the perfect choice for pushing myself off the couch, out of my robe, and into a place I would call far more "uncomfortable" than "comfortable." And because I'm an overachiever, I thought why not take it one step further, like one step out of a plane into thin air? Go big or go home, right? And so I jumped out of a perfectly good airplane with a trained professional on my back (Lord, I hope so) with only a parachute (um, just a big piece of fabric, mind you) keeping us from imminent death. Both of these crazy events I live to talk about, and write about, but I was scared out of my mind before each one. Yet, I chose to do them anyway, and they were critical parts of changing my life.

As a child, I was an avid performer. From the fireplace hearth in our living room, I spoke and sang for an audience of thousands (in my mind); it worked for me. But as I got older, I misused my gift of performing by pretending to be someone I wasn't. I made up personas and stories in an effort to fit in and be cool.

When my life changed in 2007 following my newfound relationship with Jesus Christ, I still wanted to perform. But it had to be authentic and appropriate. Hello, stand-up comedy! I could use my public speaking abilities and help people by making them laugh, right? In the end, no one in the audience threw tomatoes at me. In fact, the Improv even asked me back. Success!

While stand-up comedy was my idea of a way to get out of my comfort zone, skydiving was not. #1- I'm terribly afraid of heights. #2 – Huge reluctance to put that kind of trust in anyone, much less a stranger. However, my longtime TV producer, friend and colleague, Shana, suggested I try it. She thought it gave me a chance to help me conquer my fears in a significant way.

At that time we were filming the pilot episode of my new television series, The Janeé Show, and Shana knew my skydiving story, partnered with the strong visual content, could be a catalyst that would encourage others to tackle their own fears. For me, that jump made me a stronger person. I dealt with fear in a way I never had before and most likely won't again, by the way. I also began trusting people and their processes, which wasn't easy for me at the time. Dang! I hate when Shana's right!

If we want different results, we have to do different things. No, your next exercise does not involve jumping out of a plane or stepping up onto a stage. I'm suggesting you identify your fears and look at ways to overcome them.

Courage to Change – Exercise Five

1. List your fears. Remember, this list is for you only. Be honest and get them all off of your chest. _____

_____

_____

_____

_____

_____

_____

_____

_____

_____

_____

_____

_____

_____

2. Why does each of the fears above scare you? What exactly are you afraid of? In my skydiving example, I wasn't really afraid of height, I was afraid of trusting others and the process due to my past hurts. _____

_____

_____

_____

_____

_____

_____

_____

_____

_____

_____

_____

_____

_____

_____

_____

_____

_____

_____

_____

_____

_____

_____

_____

_____

_____

_____

_____

_____

3. For each fear above, write down steps you can take to lessen that
    fear and become "comfortably uncomfortable" with it.

    _____
    _____
    _____
    _____
    _____
    _____
    _____
    _____
    _____
    _____
    _____
    _____
    _____

4. Which of the above steps will you commit to doing and when? Be
    specific, and give yourself a deadline.

    _____
    _____
    _____
    _____
    _____
    _____
    _____
    _____
    _____
    _____
    _____
    _____
    _____
    _____
    _____
    _____

"If you always do what you've always done, you'll always get what you've always got." – Henry Ford

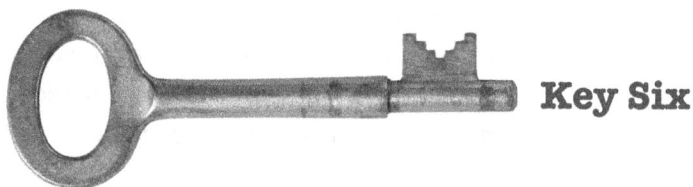

Key Six

Inside Doubts

Dear Diary,   *July 30, 2010*

I just ran into a former colleague at the grocery store. She kept asking me how I was doing and what I had been up to—over and over. It felt like an interrogation. Why was she being so nosy? Yes, I know my business is struggling right now, but my business is none of her business. Why does she keeeeeep asking me how I am? Does she know something?

The only thing this former colleague did was express interest in me and my goings-on since I'd seen her last; yet, I didn't see it that way. I took it to a dark place and jumped to all kinds of crazy conclusions. Why? Because of my inside doubts.

An inside doubt is a phrase I came up with to describe something we feel insecure about internally, but we project it externally. For instance, when this former colleague asked me how I was doing, she was simply being friendly. But I was struggling with my personal and professional lives, so it felt like an attack.

Another example is a husband who's having an affair. Let's say his wife gets a text and hubby freaks out. He wants to know who the text is from and what it's about. He might even accuse his wife of having an inappropriate relationship with this person because he's having one. He is projecting his own fears and insecurities onto her because of *his* actions, not hers.

When other people project their internal doubts on us, it's best to just let it go. Like a duck, let the beads of water roll off your back. Let it float up into the sky with the breeze. Okay, okay ... you get the idea.

At times it can be hard to decide if we're taking a statement or conversation the wrong way or if, in fact, a former colleague *is* actually being nosy and looking for dirt. Act with caution. Better safe than sorry.

When we respond irrationally to a rational question, it's a sure sign we need to step back, apologize and go back to work on ourselves by addressing an inside doubt or other area of trouble.

One area of unsubstantiated inside doubt I'm still working on is my past—the dreaded past. To this day, I'm sensitive about some of the issues I had way back when. Occasionally, when people ask me an innocent question, I give a guilty answer. When I notice I'm doing this, I take a quiet moment to remind myself I'm not who I was then. I'm growing, and I'm proud of the changes I've made and where my life is today.

Courage to Change – Exercise Six

1. Write about a time you acted defensively because of an inside
    doubt._____

    _____

    _____

    _____

    _____

    _____

    _____

    _____

    _____

    _____

    _____

    _____

    _____

    _____

2. Peel the layers of the onion and get down to the actual cause of
    this inside doubt. What is it? _____

    _____

    _____

    _____

    _____

    _____

    _____

    _____

    _____

    _____

    _____

    _____

    _____

    _____

3. Do you still need to work on this issue? If not, pick one you do need to work on. What is it, and how will you work on it? List some small steps you can take right now to help build consistent, positive change to your life.

_____

_____

_____

_____

_____

_____

_____

_____

_____

_____

_____

_____

_____

_____

_____

_____

_____

_____

_____

_____

_____

_____

_____

_____

_____

_____

"**When we are pricked by something on the outside, it is a good time to reflect what is going on inside.**" *– Janeé Hill*

Key Seven

Not My Monkey, Not My Circus

Dear Diary,   May 15, 2011

I'm proud of the changes I've made in my life, as well as the changes I'm still working on. But I'm also discouraged. I'm still butting heads with some of the people around me. The conflicts are still there. I've looked at my actions and my behaviors when one of these conflicts arises, and while I'm not perfect, I feel most of these occurrences aren't my fault. Or are they?

So, you're about halfway through this book. You've made some changes in your life for which you should be congratulated. So ... Congratulations! But I bet you still have some Downers around you, people who want to challenge whether you've really grown and changed. How can you handle these kinds of people without raising your blood pressure and sliding backward in your progress? Heck, maybe you can even help these Downers while you're at it!

First, acknowledge the elephant in the room. So many times the reason we're making changes in our lives is because we've made bad decisions in the past. Those decisions likely hurt other people or made them angry and resentful of you.

Begin by apologizing for your actions. Try to empathize with the other person's feelings; truly hear them out, and don't interrupt or become defensive. You're not offering excuses here. You're apologizing. Stay focused and calm. Your approach can be simple, but it has to be genuine. Try this: "I'm sorry for (*insert what you did wrong here*). I imagine it made you (*insert how you think it made them feel here*). Will you forgive me?" Note: The person you offended may not forgive you. That's okay. You've owned your mistake and you've offered a heartfelt apology. Those are the things you can control. You can't control the other person's reaction. This effort is about you and for you. Take what you get, be at peace with it, and move forward.

Next, be open to their reactions. It could be hurt, anger or sadness. It could be criticism, which will sting, but you probably deserve it. That's why you're apologizing, after all. Sometimes we get so focused on our own path to progress we forget to listen to other people. Let the person you offended get everything off his or her chest—within reason—and really listen. Hear that person. Often others have valuable insight on our behaviors and patterns *if* we're open to hearing them.

Finally, do not own what is not yours. Sometimes people are threatened by our progress because they know they have their own improvements to make. Instead of choosing to change and working on the issue at hand, they may lash out and play the blame game. We must thoughtfully and prayerfully consider what is ours to own and let the rest go.

Courage to Change – Exercise Seven

1. Make a list of people to whom you own an apology.

_____
_____
_____
_____
_____
_____
_____
_____
_____
_____
_____
_____
_____
_____
_____
_____
_____
_____
_____
_____
_____
_____
_____
_____
_____
_____
_____
_____
_____
_____

2   How do you think you made each of these people feel? Who do you think is still hurt, angry, sad, etc.?

_____

_____

_____

_____

_____

_____

_____

_____

_____

_____

_____

_____

_____

_____

_____

_____

_____

3.   Examine your list and see who you want to apologize to. It may not be everyone you wrote down. Reach out to every applicable person and ask for a face-to-face meeting. If that isn't possible, apologize in the most personal way you can. A phone call trumps a letter; a letter trumps an email; an email trumps a text.

_____

_____

_____

_____

_____

_____

_____

_____

_____

4. Is there anyone you think might be threatened by your improvements? How do you want to handle them from here on out? How will you set healthy boundaries?

_____

_____

_____

_____

_____

_____

_____

_____

_____

_____

_____

_____

_____

_____

_____

_____

_____

_____

_____

_____

_____

_____

_____

_____

_____

_____

_____

_____

"Looking at faults in others can delay working on the faults we see in ourselves." – Janeé Hill

Key Eight

Keeping Sane in the Insanity

Dear Diary,   *December 3, 2011*

    I can't believe it. Is this really happening? I'm pregnant, and my husband is in jail for beating me. How am I going to make it? What am I going to do? I can't even think straight. How do I get out of this true nightmare?

    Am I being punished for some of the sins of my past? Is God mad at me for everything I did years ago? If God really loved me, why in the world would He allow this to happen?

    How will I raise this child alone? What will I tell him or her about his or her father? What if he beats this little baby too??? HELP! I need HELP! I truly do not know what to do.

That is a very real diary entry. I had married a pastor, gotten pregnant on our honeymoon, and several weeks later, he was arrested. Quite the fairytale, huh? Oh, and it doesn't end there. After he was arrested for assault with bodily injury, I found out he'd been in jail before—for theft and fraud. The other shoe just kept dropping. How would I survive, much less ever thrive again? I was terrified I'd fall back into my old routines of self-destruction.

The only way to avoid that was to decide I was stronger than the temptation. Sounds easy. Bada boom! Believe me, it wasn't. It was a daily battle with myself. I found some strategies that gave me strength. I want to share them with you.

- Let yourself feel whatever it is you feel. I had faith I'd get through this apocalypse that was my life, but it certainly didn't keep me from being afraid, insecure, mad and scared. I learned to be okay feeling my emotions, but not acting on them. It was a-ok to be tomcat mad at my then husband for a bucket load of reasons, but it was not okay to beat him with a baseball bat. Yes, yes, you're right. I did itch for that lovely Louisville Slugger more than once.

- Surround yourself with people who love you. It sounds hokey, but it works. Remember me? Pregnant, newly-aware I was married to a convicted felon, and struggling with dinosaur-sized fears of having failed. Being around people was the last thing on Earth I wanted. The last thing I needed, however, was to be by myself. My dear parents and friends made sure I was always surrounded by love, literally and figuratively.

- Pray, pray, and pray some more. I honestly had no idea how this chapter in my life would end. Some days I chose not to get out of bed. My strength was non-existent, both physically and mentally. I discovered God brought me what I needed. There was a day when I didn't have the money to pay both my electric bill and buy any food. That day, someone left an ice chest on my front porch. It was packed with food. Whoever left it for me (God love them) had no idea that day I would have had to decide whether to eat or keep my lights on. At least for me, there is absolute power in prayer. I've seen it.

- PerSEVERE – Have you ever noticed that 'persevere' has 'severe' in it? Life is tough, and there is a world of hope available to us if we don't give up.

This chapter in my life ended in a way that only God could orchestrate. I delivered my son still-born on January 22, 2010. That date is a real date that I chose not to change so to honor my first-born. Four days after delivering my son, my first marriage was annulled on the basis of fraud. As tragic as all of that sounds (and believe me, it was), it was truly a blessing. It was a blessing because that child did not have to be raised in a broken, abusive home, and I was able to close the book on that chapter.

How about you? Do you have a chapter in your life that you are finished writing? If so, I encourage you to courageously open the book one more time and see what God has for you.

Courage to Change – Exercise Eight

1. Write about a difficult time you went through or are going through now. Take your time; take a break if you need one, and take it easy on yourself. This exercise could be a very difficult one._____

_____

_____

_____

_____

_____

_____

_____

_____

_____

_____

_____
_____
_____
_____
_____
_____
_____
_____
_____
_____
_____
_____
_____
_____
_____
_____
_____

2. How did you feel at the time, or how do feel now? Be specific and note why you think you felt or feel this way. _____

_____
_____
_____
_____
_____
_____
_____
_____
_____
_____
_____
_____
_____
_____
_____
_____

3. How does it make you feel to acknowledge these emotions and work them through in your head? If you need to talk about this specific situation or how you're feeling in general, do so with a friend, spouse or your breakthrough buddy. If you think this situation calls for the professional help of a therapist, psychologist or psychiatrist, find one. _____

_____

_____

_____

_____

_____

_____

_____

_____

_____

_____

_____

_____

_____

_____

_____

_____

_____

_____

_____

_____

_____

_____

_____

_____

_____

_____

_____

4. Surround yourself with people who love you. Who are they? ___

_____

_____

_____

_____

_____

_____

_____

_____

_____

_____

_____

_____

_____

_____

_____

_____

_____

_____

_____

_____

_____

_____

_____

_____

_____

_____

_____

_____

_____

_____

_____

_____

_____

5. If you're so inclined, say out loud or write a prayer about the situation you faced, or are facing. Note how you're feeling. ___

_____

_____

_____

_____

_____

_____

_____

_____

_____

_____

_____

_____

_____

_____

_____

_____

_____

_____

_____

_____

_____

_____

_____

_____

_____

_____

_____

_____

_____

_____

_____

"Heartbreaks are a part of life; they will either make us bitter or better." – Janeé Hill

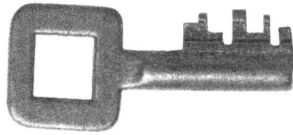

Letting Go

Dear Diary,   *July 3, 2012*

    It was a year ago today that I got married for the first time. What a disaster. I still remember that day like it was yesterday. I remember feeling like I was going to throw up on the morning of the wedding. I think perhaps that should have been my warning sign that I was not supposed to go through with the wedding.

    When am I not going to hurt from that horrendous time in my life? When will this day come and go without any recollection of the significance of that date as it relates to my marriage mayhem?

Let. IT. Go. What is "it?" "It" is whatever hurt, habit or hang-up is holding us back. Chances are, as we are reading this, we immediately think of several "its" that we need to let go of. The problem is, at least for me, that *knowing* I need to let it go is so much easier than *actually* doing it. When we have truly let "it" go, "it" no longer has power over us. "It" is a non-issue. "It" is truly in the past.

Some people say that "it" takes time. I agree with that. However, time is not all it takes.

If we are trying to get over something, the first step is to admit there is a hurt, habit or hang-up weighing us down.

Next, write out (in a safe place) the impact the hurt, habit or hang-up is having on your life. For me, I realized that holding onto bitterness, anger or resentment from my first marriage was keeping me from trusting other men and really opening the door to a new relationship.

Determine what steps you can take to move forward. For instance, see a therapist, join a support group, attend a women's retreat hosted by the fabulous author of this book (SMILE☺!).

Share your steps with a breakthrough buddy, someone you know and trust who wants the best for you and will hold you accountable for results. He or she may be one of your Upper girls or guys identified in one of the previous chapters.

Plan for progress. Take note: I said "progress" not perfection. Chances are you did not develop these hurts, habits or hang-ups overnight, and most of the time, they are not going to miraculously disappear overnight. *But* if you commit to a process, I promise, their impact will lessen. I speak from experience having overcome LOTS of hurts, habits AND hang-ups.

Courage to Change – Exercise Nine

1. List the hurts, habits, and hang-ups you are ready to let go of. Be
    honest with yourself. If you are not ready right now to let go of
    something, do not list it.

    _____

    _____

    _____

    _____

    _____

    _____

    _____

    _____

    _____

    _____

    _____

    _____

    _____

    _____

    _____

    _____

    _____

    _____

    _____

    _____

    _____

    _____

    _____

    _____

    _____

    _____

    _____

    _____

2. From the list above, list the impact each hurt, habit or hang-up is having on your life (e.g., Overeating - It is causing me to ruin my body and have health problems. It can cause me to shorten my life.)_____

_____

_____

_____

_____

_____

_____

_____

_____

_____

_____

_____

_____

_____

_____

_____

_____

_____

_____

_____

_____

_____

_____

_____

_____

_____

_____

_____

_____

3. Identify which hurt, habit or hang-up you want to work on first and list the steps you will take to start your process.

_____

_____

_____

_____

_____

_____

_____

_____

_____

_____

_____

_____

4. Who will be your breakthrough buddy? When will you talk to him or her? Recommendation: Unless the breakthrough buddy is your spouse, pick a breakthrough buddy of the same sex. It makes it much easier for accountability – trust me on this one.

_____

_____

_____

_____

_____

_____

_____

_____

_____

_____

_____

_____

_____

"Our mistakes do not define us, they refine us." – Janeé Hill

The Manifesting Mind

Dear Diary,   September 17, 2012

My actions are consistently improving, and I truly feel like I am on a solid path to being the person I want to be. However, there is one area that I am still struggling with … my mind! I swear, I feel like it is a daily battle to think positive thoughts and focus my mind.

I hear all of these motivational speakers and self-help gurus talk about the "power of the mind." But I have to say, I think my mind has the power. I mean, can we really control our thoughts? If so, what the heck does that look like? Will I ever be free of this stinkin' thinkin' that goes on between my ears???? Help!

Does anyone else struggle with a garbage drain in the brain (aka negative thoughts)? I am guessing we all do to some extent.

For me, the solution to turning my "downs" around is simple. If I want to change my mind, I have to change what I set my mind on.

Sometimes when we are thinking negative thoughts, it is because we are focusing on what *was* or what *could be* instead of what *is*. For example, a client recently reneged on a contract because he got in over his head financially. This was a significant client, and my mind immediately went to, "What will I do? I really need that income. What if I cannot provide for my family?" Clearly, I was focusing on what could be instead of the here and now. The reality is I currently have lots of projects on deck and am perfectly fine without this client's income, at the moment.

Another mental "downer" occurs when we focus on what was. Years ago, a friend made a really poor choice that greatly impacted her family. By the grace of God and through a lot of hard work, she has turned her life around. But every now and then, she gets caught up in thinking about her past, which causes her to feel shame and guilt. Focusing on what *was* will steal the joy of what *is* and is to come.

Another joy-stealer is thinking about the have-nots versus the haves in our lives. I have been through some extremely rough times financially. During those times, I often found my mind wandering to what I didn't have instead of being grateful for what I did have. Without exception, that thinking always put my mind in the gutter.

As the old saying goes, "As a man thinketh, he is." Whatever we are wanting to accomplish in life, we have to tell our mind that we can accomplish it. Otherwise, our minds defeat us before we ever get started.

Think about the person who has been overweight all of her life. If she says, "I'll never be able to lose weight," chances are, she won't lose weight. If, on the other hand, she says, "I want to lose weight, and I believe this time will be different," she has already started her mind on the right path.

Courage to Change - Exercise Ten

1. What garbage drain in the brain most resonates with you, e.g., focusing on what if, thinking about what was, concentrating on your have not's versus your have's, unbelief? List as many as apply. _____

    _____

    _____

    _____

    _____

    _____

    _____

    _____

    _____

    _____

    _____

    _____

    _____

    _____

    _____

    _____

    _____

    _____

    _____

    _____

    _____

    _____

    _____

    _____

    _____

    _____

    _____

    _____

    _____

2. Write out a specific example of when you reverted to a negative thought pattern. Re-write the scenario in a way that is focused in a positive manner. _____

_____

_____

_____

_____

_____

_____

_____

_____

_____

_____

_____

_____

_____

_____

_____

_____

_____

_____

_____

_____

_____

_____

_____

_____

_____

_____

_____

_____

_____

_____

3. What is one thing you want to accomplish in life? Write a letter
    to yourself affirming your ability to accomplish this item.

_____

_____

_____

_____

_____

_____

_____

_____

_____

_____

_____

_____

_____

_____

_____

_____

_____

_____

_____

_____

_____

_____

_____

_____

_____

_____

_____

_____

_____

_____

_____

_____

_____

_____

_____

"Out of our minds comes our attitudes, and our attitudes largely impact our actions and abilities." – Janeé Hill

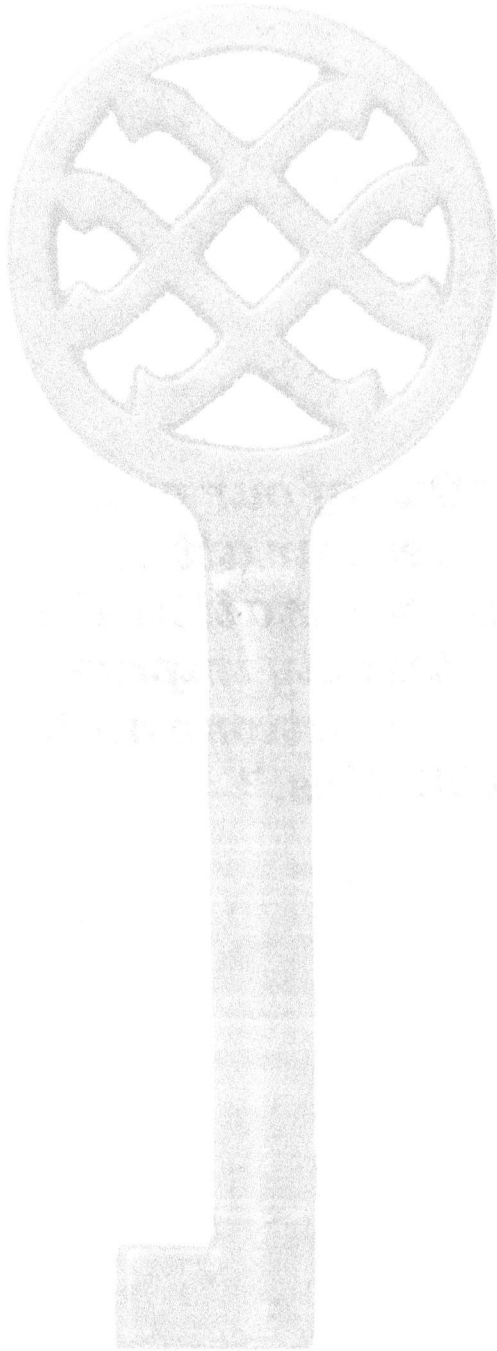

Key Eleven

Trust in God

Dear Diary,   February 2, 2013

    Stuck in my head is an awful place to be. It's like I cannot stop my wheels from spinning or my thoughts from racing. I am thinking about a lot of possible scenarios for my future, and I can't stand not knowing what lies ahead.

    People at church say, "Trust in God. He will help you figure it out." What does that mean????

    My whole life, I have always had a "plan." Granted, my plans rarely worked out as I thought they would. Nevertheless, I found great comfort in having a plan. AND every business mentor I had always strongly encouraged me to clearly lay out the path I wanted to take. Perhaps that is the problem. It has *always been the path or plan I wanted versus the path or plan that God wanted.*

So what does it look like to get out of my head and into my heart, and truly trust God to lead me???

If you are a Type A, "make-it-happen" kind of a person like me, you can probably relate to the insatiable desire to plan/figure things out *on your own.* Sure, you might "consult" God and ask for His blessing, but at the end of the day, *you* are running the show.

Not to worry, you are not alone in your control-freak conquest. I can totally relate, and it has gotten me into a lot of trouble! For instance, when I was getting married the first time, our reception venue mysteriously double-booked two weeks before the wedding. Did I take a step back and say, "Hmmm ... maybe this is a sign that I am not supposed to get married right now?" NO! Instead, I plunged ahead and wrote the local media to tell them about my wedding woes in hopes that someone would have sympathy on my reception venue mishap. Talk about taking matters into your own hands!

I would love to say this was the only instance when I went full-speed-ahead, pushing my agenda instead of seeking God's agenda, but it wasn't. I have operated most of my life taking matters into my own hands. Perhaps it is because as a small business owner I have to hustle to keep my business afloat. Maybe it is because I have been hurt in the past when I trusted people. Therefore, I feel like I have to do everything myself if I want it done right. While these might be rational reasons for doing things my way, I think they are actually tricky traps that lead to not trusting God.

Slowly, I am learning what it looks like to walk in God's will and His ways. It is so much easier said than done. However, I have learned a fairly full-proof process for trusting God and letting Him direct our steps.

1. Read the Bible - The Bible is God's Word. It is His way to communicate with us. In the past, I often had trouble

determining what God wanted me to do in a situation because I had no understanding of God's perspective. Now, I go to scriptures related to the topic at hand and seek His voice on the matter first. Note: You do not have to be a Bible scholar to make this happen. Fortunately, there are so many Biblical resources online to get you where you need to go in God's Word.

2. Pray - After we have read God's Word, we should ask Him what He wants us to do. He will show us. I am not saying He will put flashing lights on our paths or huge signs pointing in the direction we should go. But He will open and close doors when we are submitted to Him. Word to the wise: do not do what I did and beat the door down when He closes it. Trust me, that does not work out well. Ever.

3. Seek wise, godly counsel - After we have read His Word and prayed, we might want to discuss the matter with a Biblically-sound, trusted mentor. God-counsel is sometimes different than good counsel. Often, good counsel gives us sound advice, but if it is not based on God's Word, it can do more harm than good. For instance, I was debating whether or not I should give up a certain behavior. A friend of mine said, "The Bible says it's okay. I don't see what the problem is." While that may seem good in theory, there was a critical piece left out of her answer. The Bible is clear that we do not want to be a stumbling block for others. Even if this behavior is not detrimental for me, it could be detrimental for others, and the Bible is very clear about not partaking in those types of activities.

4. Listen to the not-so-still small voice - I have found that if I have 1% lack of peace about something, that is 100% of a reason NOT to do it. In the past, I looked for big glaring signs to highlight the right path for me; when in reality, all I was going to get to show me which way to go was a peace in my spirit. For me, when I am at peace, I *know* I am on the right path.

Courage to Change - Exercise Eleven

1. Write down a decision that you need to make? (It can be a large or small decision). _____

   _____

   _____

   _____

   _____

   _____

   _____

   _____

   _____

   _____

   _____

   _____

   _____

   _____

2. What does God's Word say about this matter? Note: It may not be directly related to this matter, but I guarantee you will find relevant scriptures regarding the topic at hand, if you look for them. _____

   _____

   _____

   _____

   _____

   _____

   _____

   _____

   _____

3. Who is a Godly mentor with whom you can discuss this matter?
    When will you discuss it with him or her? _____

    _____

    _____

    _____

    _____

    _____

    _____

    _____

    _____

    _____

    _____

    _____

    _____

    _____

4. What do you feel like the Lord is telling you to do? Remember:
    His ways are not our ways. I encourage you to really pray and
    ask the Lord to show you HIS will on this matter.

    _____

    _____

    _____

    _____

    _____

    _____

    _____

    _____

    _____

    _____

    _____

    _____

    _____

"Trust in the Lord with all your heart and lean not on thine own understanding. In all your ways, acknowledge Him, and He will make your paths straight." Proverbs 3:5-6

(New International Version)

Our "No's" Define Us

Dear Diary,   September 12, 2013

    I have no idea why I agreed to go to this event with Julie. The people who are going to be there are probably not the kind of people I need to be around right now. Plus, I have so much I am working on personally I need to keep my headspace clear. Nevertheless, I agreed to go. UGH!

    Also, I got an invitation to sit on a Board of Directors for a local nonprofit, and I said, "Yes." Sure, it will look good on my resume, but do I really have time to sit on another Board and be a meaningful contributor?

    I have no idea why I say "Yes" to things I really don't want to do. Am I trying to please people? Am I afraid if I say "No" that people will quit asking me to do things? What is my problem?

How many of us have said "Yes" when we really wanted to say "No?" There are many reasons we do this—people-pleasing, not sure how to say "no," pressure to fit in, desire to obtain some level of social status—the list of "reasons" goes on and on.

The problem with saying "Yes" when we are not 100% committed is that often we will come to resent what we said "Yes" to. Think about a time that you reluctantly agreed to do something. Perhaps you committed to lunch with an acquaintance and really did not want to go. Maybe you said you would take cookies for your child's homeroom class when you had absolutely no time to pull it together. How did those instances turn out for you? Chances are, they were not as good as they would have been if your desire had been a wholehearted "YES!" In fact, your life would have probably been less complicated if you had simply said "No."

Our "No's" define us. Think about that for a moment. When we say "No" to one thing, we open up an opportunity for a "Yes" with something else.

For example, I recently declined helping someone pro bono; simply because I am strapped on time between my family, career, and ministry endeavors. When I said "No" to this individual, the person was suddenly able to come up with the funds to pay me. Had I said "Yes" to this offer, I would have probably resented this person for "taking advantage" of me. When in reality, I would have been the one who allowed that transaction to occur.

When making changes in our lives, we are often striving to be something different than we have been in our past. Our "no's" will help us get there quicker and in a more focused way. I know; easier said than done. But sometimes it's better to take the advice we were given at a young age: "Just Say No!"

One final note, "No" for now does not mean "No" forever. Just because something is not right *now* does not mean that it is not right *ever*.

Courage to Change – Exercise Twelve

1. When is the last time you said "No?" How did it make you feel?

_____

_____

_____

_____

_____

_____

_____

_____

_____

_____

_____

_____

_____

_____

_____

_____

_____

2. What is something you need to say "no" to? Tell an accountability partner about your decision. Commit to a time to actually saying "No." _____

_____

_____

_____

_____

_____

_____

_____

_____

_____

_____

3. What is something(s) that you said "Yes" to that perhaps you need to re-negotiate to better align with the path you are currently on? _____

_____

_____

_____

_____

_____

_____

_____

_____

_____

_____

_____

_____

_____

_____

_____

_____

_____

_____

_____

_____

_____

_____

_____

_____

_____

_____

_____

_____

_____

_____

_____

4. What is something that may not be appropriate for right now but may be right later? _____

_____

_____

_____

_____

_____

_____

_____

_____

_____

_____

_____

_____

_____

_____

_____

_____

_____

_____

_____

_____

_____

_____

_____

_____

_____

_____

_____

_____

_____

_____

_____

_____

_____

"When we say 'No' to others, we are often saying 'Yes,' to ourselves!" *– Janeé Hill*

Key Thirteen

Keep The Change

Dear Diary,   June 24, 2014

  I am so excited! I am FINALLY seeing some changes in my life. No, my circumstances have not really changed. BUT, I am finally changing the way I respond to the circumstances, and it feels so good!

  I recently heard that a former employee said some pretty hurtful things about me. Instead of getting angry and lashing out, I calmly responded, "I am sorry she feels that way. Please tell her to come and talk to me if there is something she feels I need to work on. I would love her feedback."

  "Love her feedback???" I would have never said that in the past. Now, I am confident in the growth in my life and am ready to welcome constructive criticism if/when I need it. Wow! What a change!

  I am thrilled about what the future holds. No, there are no big business deals on the horizon or secret money trees in the works. But, there are great

things ahead, and I know that because I now have
purpose and passion, and finally, I am free from the
shame and guilt of my past. I cannot wait to share my
new-found freedom and happiness with others. I know
that in sharing my experiences, it will keep me moving
forward and becoming the woman God destined me
to be!

Wahoo!!! Change is happening! Sure, there are still areas in which we can improve, but in our hearts, we know we have made some major progress. It's time to celebrate!

"Celebrate?" you may ask. Perhaps you think it sounds cheesy, but come on, we celebrate everything else in society today. Why not celebrate the awesome changes you are making in your lives?

Here are some suggestions to celebrate your success:

1. Have a girls' night IN! – Invite your favorite friends over, put on some old movies and have each person bring their favorite movie-time snack.

2. Not-your-typical "happy" hour – Rally some friends and meet at a local charity for a "happy" hour at which happiness flows freely through your service. For instance, a group of colleagues and I met at a homeless shelter to serve dinner. It was a small act that we know left a big impression.

3. Out with the old, in with the new – Continue to shed some of the past by letting go of old clothes, pictures and accessories. Take them to a resale shop or thrift store and treat yourself to a "new" item from the store for every old gift you give.

4. Create a vision board filled with dreams and hopes for the future. Mine is full of exotic travel destinations, images from the *Extreme Makeover: The Home Edition* bus, and lots of smiling, happy people because I want to spread God's love worldwide.

In order to experience life to the fullest and obtain those items on your vision boards, you must continue to grow and "keep the change." One way I have found to do this includes helping others. When I help others, I continue to heal myself. Another way to keep growing is to join a group that gives the right vibe. It could be a small group at church, a community service organization or a women's club. No organization is perfect, so give them some grace. Finally, read God's Word and journal your thoughts. For me, the deeper rooted I am in the Bible, the more I am able to "keep my change" because I am relying on Him to help me versus doing it in my own strength.

Here's your FINAL Assignment, at least for this chapter in your book.

1. What is/are the biggest change(s) you have experienced over the past few months? _____

_____

_____

_____

_____

_____

_____

_____

_____

_____

_____

_____

_____

_____

_____

_____

_____

_____

2. How will you celebrate this change? _____

_____

_____

_____

_____

_____

_____

_____

_____

_____

_____

_____

3. How will you continue to "keep the change?" Be specific in your answer. _____

_____

_____

_____

_____

_____

_____

_____

_____

_____

_____

_____

_____

_____

_____

_____

4. With whom will you share *Diary of an Unbroken Heart?* ____

_____

_____

_____

_____

_____

_____

_____

_____

_____

_____

_____

_____

_____

_____

_____

_____

_____

_____

_____

_____

_____

_____

_____

_____

_____

_____

_____

_____

_____

_____

_____

_____

*"Brothers and sisters,
I do not consider myself
yet to have taken hold
of it. But one thing I do:
forgetting what is
behind and straining
toward what is ahead."*

Philippians 3:13

(New International Version)

The Epilogue

The Best Is Yet to Come

Dear Diary,   *June 2016*

    Wow! There is so much to tell. The past eight years have been quite the roller-coaster since choosing to do life differently and re-dedicating my life to Christ.

    2007 was probably one of the most challenging years of my life. I guess I thought that after choosing to walk with the Lord again, life would be easy ... not so much. There was a lot of damage that had been done during my "prodigal" years, and thus, there were a lot of amends or "I'm sorry's" that needed to be made. Plus, you combine that with trying to get rid of unhealthy behaviors and vices (darn those prescription meds), and life had the potential to be a recipe for disaster. Fortunately, God was with me every step of the way. He brought mentors into my life, new friends who shared similar values, and experiences that helped heal my heart and bring back some of my passions, including media!

In 2008, I went to Los Angeles to be on the show Moment of Truth that was anything but the truth. Everyone thought I was doing it for the money; I did not win a single dime. The show exploited everything I had ever done in my life and would have truly hindered my progress if a divine intervention had not occurred. Yep, that's right. A divine intervention occurred, and the show got cancelled before my episode ever aired. Thank the Lord!

From that process, I decided that instead of trying to be a light in other people's dark projects, I would start my own production company committed to authentic, positive programming designed to make a difference. Before you yawn and roll your eyes, my vision for this company was not to produce "bless your heart" cheesy, feel-good shows. Rather, it was to authentically capture the journey of life, with all of the ups and downs. From the onset, I was told a production company with this focus would "never be able to produce even one show." To all of the naysayers out there, mHe3 Productions (my production company) has produced three series that aired nationally. AND we are just getting started. The best is yet to come for mHe3 Productions; I just know it!

I would love to say that 2009 brought much success. Not so much. I was still deeply struggling with shame and guilt from my past. I felt inadequate by myself to achieve my lofty goals. So, I did what any single woman would do: I looked for a husband who could help me in life. And help he did — NOT! Unbeknownst to me, my "pastor" husband had been in jail for years for theft and fraud. To make matters worse, I had gotten pregnant on my honeymoon. Then, this lovely character was arrested for assault with bodily injury, and I was the one assaulted. Talk about a train wreck! Where were the television cameras for that god-awful reality show? Fortunately, by the grace of God, I delivered my son stillborn. As difficult as it was, I was SO thankful this happened so that I did not have to share a child with this man. My marriage was annulled on the basis of fraud four days after delivering my son, and that chapter was over. And so were my hopes and dreams for marriage and a family. However, my hopes and dreams for using media to make a difference were coming to fruition, and I produced my first television series Tour of Giving!

In 2010, I produced my second television series Revelations of Authentic Women where successful women took off the mask (using video journals) to open the door to freedom and healing. The sense of community and support that developed among the women and crew was inspiring. It planted the seed for a mobile media ministry.

I did a week-long tour of giving in 2011 (not to be confused with my first television series also called Tour of Giving). We went around the country to re-ignite the human spirit. What I found was that I still had some areas in my spirit that needed to be healed before I could move forward with any type of mobile media ministry.

I returned to Texas and launched my third television series in 2012, The Janeé Show, that was designed to walk people through a journey of faith. There were lots of unexpected twists and turns. A friend of a friend was in a tragic accident, and I delayed production to assist with the family's media needs; a long-time friend and co-worker quit midseason, and someone I esteemed a great deal betrayed my trust. "But the show must go on," as we say in the business. We produced 13 episodes and began our second season's production. But something did not feel right. Little did I know there was an unexpected "good" surprise on the way. I say "good" surprise because I have had my share of "bad" surprises in life.

In 2013, I was eating at one of my favorite restaurants Joe T's located in Fort Worth, Texas. I heard this good-lookin' guy in a cowboy hat talking loudly behind me. He was talking about a television project he wanted to produce. I gave him my card, and he said, "What if I am not interested in business?" We got married 5 weeks and 6 days later. IMPORTANT SIDE NOTE: I do not ever recommend getting married that quickly. Ever. I would love to say that it was marital bliss, but it was not. We were two broken people coming together, and marriage did not expose our "wholeness," but rather our holes. My husband had been married before, and his three daughters did not know what to think of his quick marriage. I, on the other hand, had marriage trust issues with men that erupted when put into another intimate relationship. The good news is that we are working through them. We are learning the art of good communication. And I am SLOWLY learning what it looks like to be in a blended family.

A GREAT surprise occurred in 2014: we found out we were expecting. WHOA! How did that happen? No, I am not literally asking how that happened; I am just saying that it was a totally unexpected blessing that I never dreamed possible. On August 25, 2014, I gave birth to Randal Harrell Hill. We call him RH; yes, I know, it sounds like a ranch, which seems appropriate with his father's giddy-up cowboy

tendencies. He literally is the sweetest, happiest boy –
something only God could make happen.

2015 was like the book _The Tale of Two Cities._
It was the best of times, and it was the worst of times.
It was the best of times in that we were relishing in
the joy of having a newborn. It was the worst of times
in that my entrepreneur husband had a deal go bad
that almost bankrupted us. He took a job working for
someone else, which he had not done since right out
of college. You can imagine someone who has been his
own boss for years being "bossed" by someone else.
They say, "A happy wife makes a happy home." I say,
"A happy husband makes a happy home." These were
tough times for sure. Fortunately, I had lots of work,
which helped pay the bills, and we survived (granted
we were surviving on Ramen Noodles but surviving
nonetheless).

We entered 2016 with anticipation and
excitement that a new season in our lives was ahead.
I started the year off pitching potential show concepts
to some of the big networks, which I had never done
before. It was AWESOME! We moved to the country,
and I am FAR from a country girl. Talk about a
modern day Green Acres! We continued to work on our
marriage, and slowly, we are making progress. One of
my television series, "The Janeé Show," started airing
again on Upliftv, and I finally completed my first book!

So what's next? Oh, Diary, I wish I knew.
Something tells me the best is yet to come, and the
adventure is just beginning. Get ready for the ride! It's
going to be a great one!